CONQUEROR!
NO WeaPAIN SHALL PROSPER

NIKKI CHEREE

For information, contact the Publisher:
SimplyCheree LLC
P.O. Box 651
Twinsburg Oh 44087

Editor: Angela Edwards – www.pearlygatespublishing.com

Cover Design: Kristine Cotterman – www.exodusdesign.com

Body Layout: Barbara Rodriguez – www.yayayacreative.com

Book Publishing Consultant: Lakeisha Dixon – www.lakeishadixon.com

ISBN No. 978-0-692-64711-0

PRINTED AND BOUND IN THE UNITED STATES OF AMERICA

DEDICATION

I dedicate my labor of love to you, Javis ChriShanda Dionetonette Jamison and Thomas "Tom-Tom" Lee Jefferson. Although your time with us was too short, sister and brother, you made a difference in the lives of so many. I am grateful for the times we shared together. You inspired me to live my passion and fulfill my purpose.

ACKNOWLEDGEMENTS

Thank you, Lord, for allowing the manifestation of this dream to occur. There have been many who have given words of encouragement, wisdom, support, time, and resources to bring this to pass. I am grateful and submit heartfelt appreciation to everyone who has helped me on my journey.

I extend a special acknowledgement to the following:

Family: You are so important to me – especially my children (Richara Goss, King Goss, and Nathan McCoy) who have been on the receiving end of the pain I have overcome throughout their lifetimes. I want to thank you for unwavering love and willingness to accept that you had to share the time I spent away from you with others. You are my light and inspiration. My legacy will live through you, as God blessed me with the privilege to be your mother.

Mom: Elois Jamison. You are truly the epitome of the Proverbs 31 woman. I can only hope the light reflected in me glitters at just a fraction of yours. Your voice is majestic and your strength comes from only above. I love you for being my mom and doing it diva-style. You never let me say, "I can't. I give up. I cave in. I quit." I love you dearly.

Little Brother: Clarence Jamison – I am so proud of you! Your determination to succeed is a constant reminder to never give up. Your laughter is contagious and has picked me up when I needed it the most.

Godmother: Annie Tate – Your life has shown me what it means to be a giver. Your prayers are powerfully anointed and your kindness is immeasurable. Thank you for accepting me as your daughter and loving me unconditionally.

True Love: Gary E. Odom, Sr. – Only God, you, and me knows what we have been through over the past 18 years. Our love has withstood the test of time…and everything in between. For that, I am truly grateful. You are the love of my life. I am blessed to have you as my husband.

Trusted Friends: Marian Bernard, Cynthia Carter Fuhrman, JaNeine Cunningham, and Akeya McQueen – You have seen every up and down. You have been by my side to encourage me on this journey when I was at my lowest and highest points. We are sisters, and I appreciate you for being real, true friends who would rather be honest with me than right. Thank you for holding me up and accepting me at the exact moment when everyone else turned their backs on me.

P to P Core Facilitators: Dr. Linda Wiley, Elois Jamison, JaNeine Cunningham, Bonita White, LaKeisha Dixon, Minister Delores Williams, and Pastor BJ Arnett – Each of you saw the vision God gave me and agreed to run with it. We have impacted lives together! Thank you for listening and saying "YES!" Thank you for caring and answering my call. Thank you for being a vessel to serve the needs of women. May you continue to be richly blessed with God's favor and love!

Spiritual Father: Bishop John Williams – You taught me how to value, honor, and treasure my relationship with God. From day one, you demanded a spirit of excellence in everything we do. That standard has continued with me in every area of my life. Thank you for your guidance, instruction, correction, and prayers. I pray that my life is a reflection of Christ.

Coach: LaKeisha Dixon – Nothing happens by coincidence. Thank you for allowing me to be your student and learn how to commit to my passion. May God continue to overflow you with blessings!

In Loving Memory of My Grandmother: Mattie Pope – You taught me to never lose faith. I can only imagine you in Heaven smiling and looking down on us. Your life was not easy, but you never let us know. You taught me how to be a pillar and I will love you forever.

Father God, only you know the thoughts, cares, and concerns of those who have supported me (named and unnamed). I pray you will keep them and cover them with your blood. May they have success in every area of their lives with nothing missing, nothing lacking, and nothing broken. I declare they are whole and complete, and through you, they will impact generations to come. May they walk in your divine favor and leave a legacy that will never be erased from the Earth. *In Jesus' Name, Amen.*

TABLE OF CONTENTS

FOREWORD

Our world today is filled with tremendous advances in every area, particularly medicine. I know this practice is not used much today – however, years ago when a mother gave birth to a newborn baby, the doctor would slap the baby on the bottom. The purpose of the slap was to stimulate the newborn's lungs and other organs, prompting the child to take its first breath. So, it would be fair to say that many people entered the Earth and life with slight pain; but more importantly, this pain was only given to prompt a response. Pain is only an indicator that something is misaligned or needs attention.

I am truly grateful to Nikki Cheree for her transparency after her own pain within her journey. Within the pages of this phenomenal book, you will be intrigued by the obstacles that propelled her into greatness. More importantly, Nikki unselfishly gives us a work that is a "How-To". After reading this great book, you will have the tools to navigate through pain while yielding tremendous successes!

John Williams, *Pastor*
River of Life Church
Toledo, Ohio

INTRODUCTION

There is a reason why I wake up every day: I am thankful I have a chance to get it right. What does that mean exactly? I think to myself, *"Why am I here? What have I been placed on this earth to do…to accomplish?"* Then, Heaven opens up to me and God whispers in my ear.

There is an intrinsic love I have for you –my **GOD**–sister. We are sisters who have gone through the pain and pressures of life, yet managed to overcome struggles in our own unique ways. I can relate to your story. I can interpret your tears through my experiences. I can feel your heartache because God has placed your burdens in my heart.

When God woke me up in a dream in 2009 and showed me a profile of a woman in pain, I embodied all of the attributes of abuse, low self-worth, economic hardship, domestic violence, broken homes/marriages, and damaged relationships. While I quietly suffered, I cried out to God for help and He blessed me through it. Academics, student government, sports, and music became my safe-haven…a refuge of sorts. God gave me a way to escape my pain daily. Still, I always felt second-best and not truly where I needed to be – that was until I noticed Him begin to use me in ministry.

This book tells my story and instructs you on how to recognize your pain. *What's blocking you or getting in the way? Then, once you expose it, how do you release the pain?* Give yourself permission to let go and live pain-free. Replace your energy with time spent on **Passion** – which is your gift **from** God **to** the world.

> *"For I know the plans I have for you," declares the LORD, "plans to prosper you and not to harm you, plans to give you hope and a future."*
> Jeremiah 29:11

I write this book with determination. I need to get all of this out of my heart and onto paper so you can realize the potential you have to live the whole and **completely** fulfilled life you have always dreamed of. When I say 'dream', I **am not** talking about fantasy or a fairytale life. I **am** talking about a lifestyle that is real, tangible, and within your grasp.

What I have experienced in my lifetime will be painful to some and a piece of cake to others. What I realize and know wholeheartedly is that my life's journey has allowed me to connect with many people at various levels and stages. Due to my journey, I have been *blessed* to cross many boundaries.

My prayer is that this book will allow you to identify in some way with my story and connect at a level deeper than just the words on the pages. I aspire to see a heartfelt connection that will be a catalyst for you to move from an area of 'void' to a full cup that runs **over**.

So, allow me to formally introduce myself: My name is Nikki (my name means "Victory of the people"). You may be asking yourself, *"What does that have to do with me?"* The answer is simply this: I have learned over my lifetime to move from areas of severe emotional hurt, discomfort, discontentment, shame, guilt, unbelief, and sacrifice and replaced it with a life of hope, contentment, inspiration, and joy. *I am victorious!*

Chapter 1
EXPOSE YOUR PAIN

There is an element of pain that we experience in our everyday living because we grow desensitized or get used to walking around in a struggling, numb, rat-race routine. It is important to recognize what is "normal" versus what is bondage. As with any treatment program (such as Alcoholics Anonymous), you must first acknowledge that you have a problem - whether it's addiction, depression, low self-esteem, or another area of weakness. There are many ways to walk in **P.A.I.N.** *(People, Attitudes, Insecurities, and Negative Perceptions).* I believe the devil uses pain as a weapon. John 10:10 says, *"The thief comes only to steal and kill and destroy."* We will explore the pain that can prevent you from discovering your passion; the pain that can frame your life into a box of unfulfilled purpose.

As you tackle each segment, allow yourself to identify the critical areas that need improvement or change. You will have an opportunity to write them down and begin to determine what and how to eliminate their negative effects from your life. This is a personal journey between you and God. Take your time, be honest, and lean into the discomfort. Allow your eyes to be opened and your heart to be healed.

People

A woman in pain is like a glass of champagne without any pizazz. You can fill the cup with contents, but there is not enough substance that would allow you to savor the moment by enjoying its bouquet of flavor. Nor can you reach a state of euphoria from the effect of the alcohol because there is no power from the fermentation within. Why? There is a vital, missing element; the ability for the champagne to fulfill its ***purpose***.

People have a great deal to do with your brokenness, wholeness, how you feel and/or react because you tie your relationships (or lack thereof) to them. They play a vital role in shaping and sharpening your skills to adjust to challenges, anticipate risks, and maneuver through obstacles. You need to be able to identify the individuals in your life who create pain and limit your potential. In most cases, they should be immediately removed from your intimate circle. Do not give them the privilege of having access to your God-given dreams.

Over the years, I have observed that as a woman ages and experiences life, her desire to become a people-pleaser lessens. Isn't it remarkable how when you ask an older woman who is 50+ years of age or older what she thinks about how people feel, you will almost always receive an overwhelming response of, ***"I don't care what people think!"*** I was fortunate enough to have been surrounded by a covenant of strong-willed women who cared enough to shape and mold me from infancy all the way through to adulthood.

When I think about people (in terms of pain), I realize just how critical relationships are to everyone around us. It is easy to say we don't **need** anyone - but if that was the case, why did God create us [women] in the first place. More importantly, why did God design us to have a partner in life?

As women, we are social creatures. We are natural nurturers with an innate desire to grow and develop relationships. We thrive on meeting the needs of others and having that emotional connection reciprocated. However, there is a delicate balance I believe needs to happen in our relationships. Pleasing people in the name of love can bring a lifetime of setbacks. It's important to understand why we allow people to remain in our lives close enough to influence our moods, self-esteem, or even the decisions we make. If you are to be in right-standing, **God** should be your first *love* and first relationship. ***Then*** you can truly know the real order of all other relationships and how people's roles line up accordingly.

People out of order in your life will cause you to remain in a box…frozen in a cycle of looking back - in part, afraid to move forward to achieve your goals while lacking confidence or the wisdom to change. This may seem elementary or very basic, but we often allow our emotions or needs and desires for attention *(even if it's negative)* to hold us captive.

What is preventing you from moving from where you are currently? You may be on the brink of going to the next level. You may be nowhere near the goal nor have a clue what that goal actually is! You may be in a good place...but not right where you thought you would be.

As we continue together on this journey to better understanding pain, let me share with you the profile of a woman in pain:

- Sexually abused at an early age
- Biological father was a deadbeat, alcohol and substance-abuser
- Grew up in a household with domestic violence
- Mother divorced
- Stepfather treated her different than biological children
- Sexually active early in life
- Married at a young age and experienced domestic violence in the home
- Divorced multiple times
- Single parent with no child support
- Picked up trash to make ends meet
- Received Public Assistance

- Child out of wedlock

- Had to receive counseling and therapy

- Fear of both failure and success

- People-pleaser

- Could not stand to look at herself in the mirror

As you can see from the profile, circumstances in life can have a devastating effect on you. It takes one person to love on you and make you feel 10 feet tall, but it can also take only one person to place you in a cycle of despair - not only physically, but mentally and emotionally as well. We give people the power to either add or subtract to our lives. The book *How Full is Your Bucket* by Tom Rath talks about someone adding positive deposits or deducting negative withdrawals from your spirit. This is a relationship-driven world, but how you allow the relationships to affect your plans and purpose is critical to your success.

Haters

Haters have a spirit of competitive ***jealousy***. Why? Simply because they see in you what they either want for themselves and cannot obtain, or they judge the blessing in your life versus their own. Haters are sold out on the idea of you failing so they can get some form of satisfaction or gain from your demise. Often, they will be the ones who are more vocal and challenge your position, success, and/or accomplishment at any stage. When you share your most intimate ideas or thoughts with haters, they will compare them to their own. This can result in their plagiarism and ultimately untimely exposure or sabotage. Haters take your success personally and have no qualms about reminding you of how you *used* to be, act, talk, and walk prior to any level of success.

How do you deal with haters? You cut off access. Haters aren't without purpose. They are in your life to force you to think or anticipate risks and come up with solutions. They test and try you. As described in James 1:1-4, *"Consider it pure joy, my brothers and sisters, whenever you face trials of many kinds, because you know that the testing of your faith produces perseverance. Let perseverance finish its work so that you may be mature and complete, not lacking anything."* Tests and trials push you to relinquish your will to God. They help you recognize the value of **true** friendships – which are few and far between.

You may have heard the phrase, *"If someone is talking about you, then you must be doing something right."* Let me be clear: You do **not** have to keep haters in your life. Let them go. If you find them constantly in the mix, stay cool and focused. Their words, slander, and degradation may hurt, but what *God* says about you is far more important.

At the times in my life when the haters seemed most toxic, I would go into the bathroom and look in the mirror. I would declare the following: *I am the head and not the tail. I am more than a conqueror. I believe in me.* Over and over and over again, I would force myself to make those declarations - even when the reflection in the mirror was not who I wanted or expected to see.

Takers

The equivalent of a thief, blood-sucker, or leech is a *taker*. These types of people (like haters) recognize your potential, but they seize the opportunity to be connected so they can take advantage of your grace, favor, and blessing. They will always be in the background promoting their loyalty, but they don't ensure that when you are close to the ditch, you don't fall in. If they can benefit, they will be right there with you. These are your "homies" or *(in the most common example from the church)* takers are the chickens that like to hang with the eagles. Takers can be your boyfriend, family member, business partner, coworker, or so-called best friend. When you eat, they eat. The **problem** is that they lack vision and motivation of their own, so they suck the essence from you. As you elevate, they also want an elevated status...but their *mindset* remains the same.

When you cut off a taker, they *instantly* become haters. Sure, they may have helped you along the way or even thrown you a couple of bucks, but their investment does **not** require a lifetime of dividends as payback. I acknowledge that during the journey, you should have a heart to serve - but understand that manipulation and pity will be used against you to keep you tied to trying to save everyone else around you.

Takers are in your life as a distraction. Their presence should sharpen your ability to discern not only their motives, but your intentions as well. Why do you have takers around you? Is it because you desire to feel needed or in control of another? Do you need to feel a sense of accomplishment via taking care of others? In many self-help circles, it is said that if you are the highest rung in your circle, then get up off your stepstool and create a new circle!

Whether it's your man, mother, or best friend, a taker will *always* feel entitled to your stuff. Why? Because at some point, you gave them the power to make you feel obligated or beholden to them. You carry the burden of looking out for their well-being and they become a permanent appendage…dependent on you. Unfortunately, the only way to remove the appendage is to cut it off. That in itself can be a painful process. Letting go of being an enabler for someone who takes from you is not easy - even though that seems ironic.

I think about the number of times I was called late at night to provide a temporary fix for someone. The support requested was for help - usually emotional. What did I do? I jumped into encourager, intercessor, and exhorter mode. I used all of my energy and focus to help them get over the hump, get a job, make it through a relationship crisis, or even paying their bills. When it was time for me to deal with my **own** stuff, I was depleted - and they were unable to provide anything in return. *The airline industry warned me about such things: I gave them my oxygen before first breathing in for myself.* As long as you're giving, they are taking. Don't die prematurely for someone who will never be satisfied.

Fakers

In this society of microwaveable instant oatmeal versus slow-cooked grits from a stovetop, it's hard to tell what's authentic. Fakers are really good imitators of everything you thought you would ever want or need. The role of a faker is to deceive you so that your dreams and ambitions can be destroyed. They know how to get close and become your best friend and the lust of your life (*notice that I did not say **love***). As you give them your intimate treasure, they slowly plant seeds of doubt and negativity because they are chameleons. They change with every situation. Ultimately, they are haters **and** takers. Growing up in church, when it came to finding a **good** man, my pastor would say that the devil will send you a counterfeit…so wait on God to send you who you *really* need.

Fakers display signs of not being genuine. When you wonder how your idea got stolen or was prematurely revealed, don't look far: Look closely at those around you. You will learn to listen to your gut and follow your instincts. The small whisper of the Holy Spirit will warn you whenever fakers are in the vicinity. Don't make the mistake I made and convince yourself that the snake next to you really *isn't* a snake dressed up like a six-foot, medium-build, muscular man with shiny white teeth… and **NO JOB**! Turn around and run! I've been down some shady paths trying to run in lanes with fakers. The song lyric is accurate when it says, *"They smile in your face and all the while they want to take your place - the backstabbers."*

Waiters

Waiters are your critics 'from afar'. For the most part, waiters may be people in positions of influence (i.e. parents, mentors, or even a spouse). You really desire their support and approval. The waiters are the "they" people often refer to in conversations. Their reactions can make or break belief in yourself, your confidence, or your self-esteem. Typically, waiters are skeptical and try to shape the box you live in by "keeping it real" with you. They say things like: "Stay in your lane", "It doesn't take all of that", and "Stop trying to be like the Joneses". They have no ability to understand just how big the vision is that God placed inside of **you**, so they downplay it with an 'I'll believe it when I see it' attitude.

The waiter's role in your life is to help you truly recognize where your provision, power, and authority comes from. Waiters can be a potential help to you (i.e. an investor or sponsor) but will eventually disappoint you. ***God's*** love for you will **never** fail. Scripture says, *"Love never fails. But where there are prophecies, they will cease; where there are tongues, they will be stilled; where there is knowledge, it will pass away"* (1 Corinthians 13:8 NIV). Waiters in your life are designed to test your faith, toughen your resolve, and give you strength to say "**NO**" and move on.

Waiters keep themselves at a distance and often fall out of your life on their own. At the time, you may see them as your short-term fix and suffer disappointment. They become your dream-snatchers, but **God** is a *permanent* solution. Your will to press on - coupled with a heightened sense of determination - will outweigh those distant naysayers by a longshot!

LADIES, STOP GIVING AWAY YOUR STUFF! Allow the seeds to be sown from those who are genuine and are not raping you of your treasure… the ones who are not stealing your jewels, pillaging the best of you, and using you as a dumpster. We were designed with a womb. We take the fertilized seed and we multiply. We give birth to whatever deposits we have received. What are you birthing? What (or who) are you allowing to grow, feed off of you, or suck the very essence out of who you are to allow *them* sustenance?

NOTES

_____

_____

_____

_____

_____

_____

_____

_____

_____

_____

_____

_____

_____

_____

Attitudes

Have you ever heard the phrase, "Your attitude determines your altitude"? Dr. Miles Munroe (a notable author, spiritual leader, and expert on leadership) says that we need to maximize our potential. What does *that* mean? It means you will only go as high, far, expand as broad, and go as deep as your mind will take you. Attitude means: Are you conscious of the way you think and feel about what happens to you – *because of you*? What frame of mind do you have when you wake up in the morning? What about when you lay down at night? Is your early mindset the same when you end the evening late? Do you blast someone who makes a mistake or do you love on them and help them learn how to overcome? Has the way you have been treated, overlooked, praised, celebrated, tainted, or stimulated affected how you make decisions? Are you a victim? A pessimist? What part of your attitude needs adjusting? Attitude impacts **everything** you do. It determines your outlook. It frames the picture you see. Some say, "What a beautiful portrait the Mona Lisa is!" How much do you think the *frame* surrounding her picture is worth? Would the Mona Lisa have as much value without the frame?

I have taken a lot of time to self-reflect about the effects attitude has on passion. What I have come to realize is that our attitudes are completely controllable elements. They are driven by our emotional state of mind coupled with the things we allow to take precedence in our mind. For example, I made the decision to cut my hair when I turned 40. I believed I was going to "rebuild myself" and come up with a whole new look. I began to think on this fact in terms of my overall fabulousnesses. I thought about how I was going to change my image and come up with a new look in terms of my appearance. I had a focused attitude and perspective around my hair. It had taken me quite some time to grow it out as it was - and I already looked good! I felt good, too. My attitude about myself was positive. Nonetheless, how I envisioned myself at 40 was important to me.

In the meantime, leading up to the transformation, I decided to go 'natural'. Subsequently, my hair began to fall out and I ended up *having* to cut it because it was damaged. That changed my entire attitude. I lost confidence and a sense of self-value. Why? I had focused so much on future things that I began to make decisions in the present that negatively impacted my goal. My attitude was less about what was really important in terms of my self-worth and more about things that didn't really matter.

We control our attitudes, ladies. We have the power to allow someone else (or ourselves) to impact them. The most important thing to remember is that we make conscious choices and decisions. If we choose to allow to be taken in the wrong direction, we can also choose to come out of whatever slump or hole we find ourselves falling in to.

Our attitudes come from deep within us. As we think about money, relationships, family, and careers, our experiences with those things affect our attitudes. For example, if we convince ourselves that our bosses are out to get us, then we will have a negative attitude towards that person or maybe even the job. *What would happen if we changed our frame of reference?* We could create a very different reality for ourselves!

Relationships play a big part in our attitudes. For example, do you spend a lot of time with people who believe they cannot get a fair shake in life or that "the man" keeps passing them over? Do you think your husband is cheating on you or doesn't love you anymore? How do you feel about whether the kids love you or not because you are a single mother? As you reflect on the various aspects of your life, what is your attitude? Are you honest about your feelings? Can you express your real hurt and discomfort with yourself *first*? If the answer is no, then you may have a negative attitude about yourself.

How do you change your attitude in a way that creates power? Let's focus on four areas:

1. Realize your truth is different than someone else's.

2. Understand you have the power to control your attitude.

3. Acknowledge that your destiny is wrapped in the attitude you have towards your life's plan.

4. Recognize feelings are temporary.

Realize your truth is different than someone else's.

Oftentimes, we grow up wanting to please someone else. Our attitudes about accomplishment are shaped by the praise (or lack of) we received while very young. If you have not been in a position to receive a lot of praise, it's okay. You can learn to create small victories for yourself. A solid sense of progress will lead to a better sense of purpose - which will lead to more passion. As you dig deep and begin to face the harsh realities of your life and the areas that are holding you back, you will see you can begin to change your attitude. Shame, guilt, frustration, envy, jealousy, hurt, and brokenness lead to negative attitudes.

When someone calls you out of your name or says you are not good enough, that is their way of transferring their negative attitude onto you. Don't believe the hype! Constructive feedback is supposed to be just that: *constructive*. Anything that does not give you grounds to rebuild, capitalize, or improve, you can throw away. Feedback is a gift only if it is useful.

One trap I have fallen into is valuing the opinions of mentors over my own self-worth. I thought that mentors had the final say. What I have since learned is that they are sounding boards. Mentors have their **own** set of values and attitudes about the decisions you need to make. Always choose mentors who have a variety of different experiences, are truthful, and align with your core beliefs. No one can determine your reality unless you *allow* them to. You must relinquish that power to them first. *I advise against doing so.*

Understand you have the power to control your attitude.

Every day that you awake is an opportunity for a fresh start. You are able to reflect back on your setbacks and accomplishments – and then make adjustments. The way you interpret your failures will be the key to your success. Keep in mind that God placed you on this Earth with a purpose. He gives you power through His Spirit.

"You were taught, with regard to your former way of life, to put off your old self, which is being corrupted by its deceitful desires; to be made new in the attitude of your minds; and to put on the new self, created to be like God in true righteousness and holiness."

(Ephesians 4:22-24)

One way to control your attitude is to repurpose, replace, and reposition things that are out of order in your life.

Acknowledge that your destiny is wrapped in the attitude you have towards your life's plan.

In my professional life, I spent a lot of time sharing with people that my work did not define who I am as a person. I would make statements like, "My job is a means to an end. It is a part of my life's plan." In the early stages of adulthood, I learned the concept of visualization. I applied the rule: ***"Write your vision down and make it plain."*** I clearly remember developing collages that depicted my life. They went something like this:

There were four corners representing:

- Career-minded business woman;
- Education;
- Mother; and
- Healthy lifestyle.

In the center of my collage was the Earth with hands wrapped around it. That was indicative of my faith and belief that God had everything in His control and was the center of my life. I can vividly remember some of the pictures I had cut out of magazines. Then, I made personal goals and commitments to myself regarding what I was going to do to make those pictures of success a reality. The collage became my life's plan. Although I lost that collage many years ago, the images are still burned in my mind. I often reflect back on the things I have accomplished since making that collage…

As I entered the professional and business parts of my life, I struggled with ensuring that I remained focused on the center. Was my life still aligned with God being in control? Was I straying from my purpose in life? What was my purpose? I asked myself those questions many times over – then began the journey of identifying my purpose and living it out.

What I have found most fulfilling is that my job has become a platform for living out my purpose. It does not define who I am, but it **does** help me to become a better me. There have been many lessons learned. My territory has expanded in terms of the people whom I have touched and those who have impacted me. I have never regretted my small beginnings…

Recognize feelings are temporary.

This is an area where women get trapped, stuck, road-blocked, bamboozled, and hoodwinked! We allow our feelings to rule. Ladies, your feelings are driven by emotion. Feelings are dynamic…they change, just as the seasons change. No two thunderstorms are the same. It is the same with our feelings. We can be mad at our mate one day and love him the next. The important thing to remember is that your attitude can also be impacted.

As I write my thoughts, I realize how long it has taken me to get here because of my **own** pain. Over the years, I would tell people that I was an overcomer because I have lived a life of adversity – and that is a true statement. *However*, what is **equally** true is that overcoming adversity was comprised of a series of choices and decisions that had to be made at critical points in my life. You cannot *wish* a problem away. Although prayer changes things, *action* is required.

What I found is that as I became more specific with God in devastating situations, God had something for me to do. Standing in the midst of the storm did not mean I did not take cover. I was afraid, but I had to ensure I was prepared for the next wave that was going to hit. In addition, as I grew older, I was no longer responsible for just myself. Unfortunately, I had allowed my children to be dragged into my painful situations because of the choices I made along the way. I felt guilty. The saying,

"Misery loves company", held true in my life. My children were innocent bystanders learning what **not** to do as I gave my power, strength, and life away to someone else. God is faithful; I was not. Glory to God! He showed me that I did not have to stay in a place of shame and guilt because of what I allowed in my life or my children's lives. I was *finally* able to move from **pain** to **purpose**.

NOTES

_____

_____

_____

_____

_____

_____

_____

_____

_____

_____

_____

_____

No WeaPAIN Shall Prosper–CHEREE

Insecurities

I once asked myself, *"What makes me feel insecure?"* My answers spewed onto the page immediately: family, religion, fear of judgement, fear of failure, fear of rejection, fear of abuse, and loss of power. I was able to articulate the grip that insecurity has had in my life without hesitation. I was used to living in that box for so long, insecurity had become a part of my existence.

Ladies, our struggle with insecurity connects to our sense of purpose. When you build a house in order to ensure it can weather a storm, it has to have a solid foundation. Some of us have not had the luxury of having a solid foundation…but that doesn't mean it's over. What you absolutely cannot worry about are the insecurities you feel or those of someone around you. Often, someone else may feel intimidated or jealous of what you have to offer and that fuels your own insecurity - **BUT** know that your gift makes room for you. There is enough infinite space, wealth, and success to go around for everyone. Be conscious to not allow someone to transfer what their hang-ups are on to you.

I know what it feels like to lose myself in the pain of insecurity. As a child, I was outgoing, willing to take risks, and ready to try new things. Over time - through sexual abuse, domestic violence, and the lack of my father in my life - I became more withdrawn and learned to incubate myself from pain. I would play in the closet and had developed an array of "imaginary friends" who took on different personalities. For example, 'Ola Ray' was the beautiful, successful woman who would model, sing, and was an actress. 'Margaret' was the intelligent business woman. They were the characters I sought refuge in for years to help me through terrible situations.

You might ask, *"Why did Nikki share that so openly?"*

I look back now and realize that my defense mechanism helped me replace the insecurities with ***positive*** images in my mind so that I could continue to function and excel. No one knew my secrets, hurts, and desires outside of God and my closest friends. When I entered my young adult stage, those friends were no longer able to shield me from my pain. I was making bad choices and decisions under the guise that no one would ever be able to take advantage of or hurt me again. I was going to maintain power and control over my life. *I never realized that was insecurity at its best.* I turned to men, sex, and even my education as my refuge. The more thuggish the man, the more attracted to him I was. Their hard demeanors inspired me to prove that I was tough, too. If I could match them physically and verbally, then I was in control. I used my education as a shield of protection because I was smart and could out-talk anyone in my vicinity. The severity of my insecurities was ever-growing.

The cycle of generational curses began to repeat themselves in my life. In the midst of my marriages, domestic violence, guilt, and shame, I met Jesus Christ - my Lord and Savior. I slowly began to replace my insecurities with faith, love, advocacy, and joy.

> *"And I heard a loud voice from the throne saying, "Look! God's dwelling place is now among the people, and He will dwell with them. They will be His people, and God Himself will be with them and be their God. He will wipe every tear from their eyes. There will be no more death or mourning or crying or pain, for the old order of things has passed away." He who was seated on the throne said, "I am making everything new!" The He said, "Write this down, for these words are trustworthy and true."*
>
> Revelation 21:3-5

Realizing that God had a purpose for my life began to lower the impact of insecurity. As I began to acknowledge that my wisdom, knowledge, provision, advancement, and favor came from God, it then became less about what I was missing in life. The sting of rejection from my biological father was nullified because my Heavenly Father was always there to comfort me. I began to understand why my mother named me 'Nikki' - which (again) means "Victory of the people".

At various stages of our lives, we will experience insecurities in some way, shape, or form – whether in the family, on the job, in church, or in business. They key is to move from them and not allow them to cause you to become paralyzed and stay stuck. Be open and honest with yourself about what concerns you. Know that **FEAR** (*False Evidence Appearing Real*) is often us making up in our minds the worst possible scenario of what *could* happen before anything actually manifests. The first step is to identify what you are most insecure about and give those issues to God. You must be truthful and honest with yourself and trust God to show you the way through.

NOTES

_____

_____

_____

_____

_____

_____

_____

_____

_____

Negative Perceptions

What is your self-image and self-worth? How do you value yourself? How would you rate your life on a scale of 1 to 10?

Negative perceptions can be dangerous because they are silent and run deep. Life is shaped by our experiences, trials, successes, failures, and how we were reared as children. HOWEVER, your negative perception is a **LIE**. Couple that **LIE** with **HATERS** and you could be treading on dangerous ground. Why? Because sometimes people identify or see you differently because of *their* frame of reference – not for who you really are. Your job is not to convince them otherwise, but to stay the course. Be true to you and succeed in every area of your life. Everyone is not going to be able to "go there" with you. You have to view yourself in a way that makes you remarkable. Do you realize you are extraordinary in your everyday, ordinary life? The things that you have and the way you "do you" cannot be matched, measured, or remixed. You are an original! Don't fall into the trap of seeing yourself from the LIARS' and HATERS' points of view. Speak truth and be true to who you are and were created to be.

Insecurities fuel negative perceptions from the inside out. They can do the most damage because if you believe you are who "they say" you are, then the battle is already lost…in your mind.

When I think about my own struggles with negative perceptions, I can remember how I felt back in middle school. I had a principal whose slogan was: "If you believe, you will achieve." I took that to heart, so I worked hard on academics, sports, and music. I was on the Honor Roll and was oftentimes the only Black child in my classes. One day, a teacher told me I was not *really* Black. I did not understand what he meant. He went on to further explain that I was not a 'typical' Black student because I did not have the "Black experience"...simply because I played the violin, was in Honors classes, and was privileged. I can remember how angry and hurt I was at the time because when I went home, I lived in an urban area, had to take the city bus to get to school, and was being raised by a single mother. His willingness to label me in front of all of my classmates was confusing – especially since in my neighborhood, the kids said that I acted White because of the proper way I spoke. They labeled me as being a nerd. It was a very confusing time in my life. I had so many images of who I was *not*, I had difficulty understanding who I *was*. *All of the perceptions were wrong.* I can remember sobbing and asking my mom the question, "Who am I?" She smiled, lifted my chin up off her lap, and said, "Baby, you are the head and not the tail – a child of God." Those words have remained with me to this very day.

I began to understand that negative perceptions are visualizations of how we see ourselves both inwardly and outwardly. As women, we invest time on what we look like to others - our *image*. We strive to paint pictures of happiness, economic status, attractiveness, etc., yet work is rarely done on improving our intrinsic value.

You may be struggling **right now** and can't figure out how to make ends meet, but your true value comes from the fruit you bear. Your wealth is not determined by your status or how willing you are to give away your jewels. No matter what it looks like - whether you are rich or poor, slender or obese, fair-skinned or dark-skinned - you are **exactly** who God created you to be. Although we are bombarded with images and attacks from characters in our lives, the best offense is to put your trust in God and remain steadfast.

> *"Then you will win favor and a good name in the sight of God and man. Trust in the Lord with all your heart and lean not on your own understanding; in all your ways submit to Him, and He will make your paths straight."*
> Proverbs 3:4-6

There is no perfect person alive today. In all of our imperfections, the most valuable creation exists - and that's **you**! Ladies, I am here to let you know that you are *more* than **ENOUGH**. Take off the mask you wear on the job. Remove the dishonor you feel if you're broken in this moment. Negative perceptions are temporary and can be replaced. Remember always: They do not define you.

There is a process that a caterpillar goes through in order to become a butterfly. It all happens away from the naked eye. From the outside it looks like nothing is happening, but the work is still being done. Don't underestimate your process. Once you become a butterfly, it will only last for a season…and then your process will start all over again.

NOTES

_____

_____

_____

_____

_____

_____

_____

_____

_____

_____

Chapter 2
UNVEIL YOUR PASSION

D o you have a burning desire that excites you at the very moment it crosses your mind? Does it excite you to the point that it incites you to act or accomplish a goal? Have you ever wanted to push or fight to the finish so bad just because others said they didn't believe in you or that your 'something' could not be done? Have you ever earnestly prayed to God that you did not want to die and leave this world without fulfilling your purpose?

Ladies, your passion is constantly pressing you. It does not cease when times are hard. Neither does it coast when times are good. Your passion is constantly telling you to progress and add more to your life. In fact, passion is a fire that is fueled from deep within. It is the force that keeps your purpose in the forefront of your mind and propels you towards the actions that are necessary to bring it to fruition.

Mel Gibson's movie, *The Passion of the Christ*, exemplifies Jesus Christ's passion and commitment to fulfill His purpose. Christ's purpose was to save us and the world despite all adversity! Passion never dies… unless you allow the fire to be diminished. It never fails…unless the environment is not conducive to promoting an increasing fire, energy, and drive.

As we continue on this journey to better understand passion, let me share with you the profile of a woman living her dream:

- Honor roll student

- Student Council

- Varsity Athlete

- Talented Musician

- Earned graduate degree

- Obtained internships beginning in high school through college

- Married with children

- Works at a Fortune 500 company

- Recognized with various Awards for achievements

- Six-figure income

- Entrepreneur

- Nice home, car, goes on family vacations

- Confident

- Able to give back to her community

- Ministry

Think about the woman who was just profiled. Compare and contrast her to the profile of the woman in pain in Chapter One:

- Sexually abused at an early age
- Biological father was a deadbeat, alcohol and substance-abuser
- Grew up in a household with domestic violence
- Mother divorced
- Stepfather treated her different than biological children
- Sexually active early in life
- Married at a young age and experienced domestic violence in the home
- Divorced multiple times
- Single parent with no child support
- Picked up trash to make ends meet
- Received Public Assistance
- Child out of wedlock
- Had to receive counseling and therapy
- Fear of both failure and success
- People-pleaser
- Could not stand to look at herself in the mirror

Which one of these women would **you** rather be? You may find yourself relating to one more than the other; however, I submit to you today that whether you are similar to Woman #1 or Woman #2, you *can* move from **PAIN** to **PASSION**. Why am I so confident? Because both profiles make up one person: ME!

I know you may feel like life is overwhelming you at times, but you will **never** take on more than you can bear. Make a commitment to throw away your **PAIN**. Spend your time, energy, and efforts pouring your heart into your **PASSION**. Why am I taking the time to share this with you? Because I love you. Because you are important. Because you matter.

We are living in a dangerous time, ladies. I'm not referring to pandemics, floods, or the failing economy. We are in a dangerous time because the world is in jeopardy of missing out on **your** gifts and talents; **your** solutions to the world's problems. We cannot afford to allow our seed – the next generation – to have to pick up the pieces and complete the puzzle. How long will **you** make us suffer? How long must we wait before **you** say *"YES"*?

The first step to living your passion is making a commitment to **Exit** your pain, **Enact** your gifts/talents, and **Embrace** your passion. I take this step so seriously, we are going to take a pause and allow you time to reflect.

Take some time to consider those things that come naturally to you with ease. What do you do in excellence that flows effortlessly from your innermost to outermost? Where is your best self 'reflected'? Where have you hurt the most or suffered the greatest loss and want to do something about those feelings? What will cause you to jump through hoops in order to get it done, even if alone? What makes your heart flutter and creates the internal song of your life? Capture those areas where you feel your life will make the most impact. This is not an exercise in volume or quantity...but *quality*. Do not look through the lens of what's large or small. Look at only what is good and can be done from your heart with love. Love will motivate and inspire you to overcome.

When you have reflected upon those things, then you will be able to fully capture your commitment on paper. Habakkuk 2:2-3 reads, *"And the Lord answered me, and said, Write the vision, and make it plain upon tables, that he may run that readeth it. For the vision is yet for an appointed time, but at the end it shall speak, and not lie: though it tarry, wait for it; because it will surely come, it will not tarry"* (KJV).

Once you write down your commitment, you have released your destiny to fulfill its purpose in the earth. Do not be afraid! Things will seem overwhelming and even hectic at first. Do not worry. As verse 4 of the aforementioned passage continues, *"Behold, his soul which is lifted up is not upright in him: but the just shall live by his faith"* (KJV).

My best results were achieved when the heat was turned up in my life. Once you make a commitment, the characters of pain will gear up for the press. Just remember: Passion is like a pot of boiling water. At first, the water remains still until the heat is applied. Once the fire is lit underneath, the process begins of slowly intensifying – causing you to act and move forward. That, ladies, is a very crucial time. Why? Because it is at *that* point when you can change your mind and become unfocused about your intentions, decisions, or expected outcomes.

All too often in my life, I decided to quit before the fire became too hot…

Ladies, listen up: You cannot afford to lose your motivation just because the heating process takes some time. At first, only a few air bubbles may surface (*similar to how we come to the realization of who we are in Christ and walk in the calling that has been placed on our lives*). The people may only just begin to see where your passion is taking you. Just know that a rapid boil is quickly approaching where the fire is **hot** and the anointing can flow freely. Then look at the results! Don't allow *PAIN* to turn down your fire!

Let's begin by completing the following personal contract…to yourself. This is for you to keep. Sign and date it. Then give yourself a round of applause because you have taken your first step to moving away from your **Pain** and living a life of **Passion**!

Exit / Enact / Embrace Contract

Father God, I have made a quality decision to *Live My Passion* and walk in the manifestation of what **YOU** have already done in my life! I commit to seek your face, obey your instruction, and take action according to your Word. I no longer accept defeat because of the *PAIN* I have allowed to overshadow the purpose **YOU** have given to me. I declare that I am an overcomer and see myself as you see me. I thank you for the wisdom, knowledge, and understanding to know that I am yours...**I AM FREE** to live a life of **purpose**. Today...

I EXIT *my pain:*

P. _____

A. _____

I. _____

N. _____

I ENACT *my gifts / talents:*

1. _____

2. _____

3. _____

I EMBRACE *my passion:*

1. _____

2. _____

3. _____

Father, I commit to remain diligent and consistent as I walk out my journey. In **YOU** and through **YOU**, I will positively impact the lives of your people. I decree that your will be done and that you receive *ALL* of the glory. I will not give up, cave in, or quit! Thank you, Lord: **I AM VICTORIOUS**, in Jesus' Name.

Name:_____

Date: _____

NOTES

_____

_____

_____

_____

_____

_____

_____

_____

_____

_____

_____

_____

_____

_____

_____

_____

_____

_____

_____

No WeaPAIN Shall Prosper–CHEREE

Chapter 3
TAKE OFF THE MASK
AND BREATHE

Over the past year (before penning this book), I had experienced a lot of changes and loss: divorce, the deaths of my sister and grandmother, a new job, relocation from one state to another, and a host of new relationships all around me. I asked God, *"How, Lord, am I supposed to know my purpose and fulfill your will when I am physically and emotionally spent?"* I struggled to think straight and keep up with the pace of changes, but I also knew I had to go on in spite of the heartache, tragedy, and pain. I **know** what I am most passionate about, but life seems to continue to get in the way!

It was then that I realized moving forward was going to take time. Moving from ***pain*** to ***passion*** is a journey... it's a process. Things may not suddenly change for you overnight. If we are truly going to be who God has called us to be and live out ***His*** purpose for our lives, then we have to make some real, deliberate, and conscious decisions. Although there may negative circumstances along the way, they will not take you away from God's design and purpose.

> *"For I know that nothing can keep us from the love of God. Death cannot! Life cannot! Angels cannot! Leaders cannot! Any other power cannot! Hard things now or in the future cannot! Any other living thing cannot keep us away from the love of God which is ours through Christ Jesus our Lord."*
> Romans 8:38-39

Picture this scenario: An athlete is preparing for the New York Marathon. Her boss tells her that she will pay one million dollars to said athlete if she represents the company well *and* wins the race. How many of you think you would able to accomplish that task? For one million dollars, many of us would be able to do just about anything, right? But think about it: You may be motivated to run the race...but are you equipped to win? Do you have stamina? Do you possess the necessary conditioning, training, and mental attitude to keep going when your legs start to burn or your faith starts to falter?

That's what God is asking you. As a Christian, you know there is a great reward at the end of this life's race - but how equipped are you to handle the charge that He has personally given you? For example, if you are called to speak at a 3-day conference, can your body handle the outpouring and release of His spirit or will you fall out because your body is not conditioned to handle the anointing of God that is being released from you? How about singing on the Praise and Worship Team and you get tired after the second song...when the entire service becomes one powerful praise and worship service with no preaching? Romans 12:1 reminds us: *"Therefore, I urge you, brothers and sisters, in view of God's mercy, to offer your bodies as a living sacrifice, holy and pleasing to God – this is your true and proper worship."*

This chapter is designed to explain what we can do to maintain our physical, mental, and emotional aspects while walking our *spiritual* journey.

The first step is always the hardest when you want to achieve a goal. New Year's Day is filled with resolutions from everyone making commitments to lose weight, read more, pray more, and spend more time with family. The **results** are usually less than what we desire them to be because there was not enough motivation to endure.

As I studied the Word of God and conducted *Pain to Passion* workshops, I have found that this section was always a great hit with the ladies. The workshop allowed the participants to become transparent in an atmosphere of intimate fellowship. It set the stage for opening up and exposing some of their hurts and deepest desires while really grasping the practical concepts required to move forward. It instilled in each participant that taking care of the physical body is necessary in their journey. It allowed small successes and wins to be identified and gave the ladies permission to breathe and take a rest. Finally, participants committed to loving themselves and have learned practical ways to cope.

Let's dive deeper into a few of those elements.

Become transparent in an atmosphere of intimate fellowship

The goal is to create an atmosphere of worship where the presence of God could saturate the room and your heart and mind would be clear of everything. That setting is critical to enable the downloads and outpouring of creativity to occur. That meant that at designated points throughout the day, week, month, and year, you would be clear to separate yourself from business. Preferably, you would escape to a quiet room or location and meditate on God's Word, receive instruction from Him, and submit your will. It is a time of refreshing and renewal because there should be no distractions.

> *"If my people, who are called by my name, will*
> *humble themselves and pray and seek my face*
> *and turn from their wicked ways, then I will*
> *hear from Heaven, and I will forgive their*
> *sin and will heal their land."*
>
> 2 Chronicles 7:14

During this time, you will receive clarity of vision and expansion. Seek God and He will give you answers. Trust Him and acknowledge what He has already done. Reverence Him and see the manifestation of His power in your life.

God is the source of **every** good thing in my life. I have dedicated time with God to get in His presence. Sometimes, I just lay on the floor and listen. Other times, I play worship music and pray out loud. There are times when I will journal and write down what He places in my heart. There are many ways to be in His presence. The key is to do it. Do not take for granted that your first relationship *should be* with your Heavenly Father. His love for you is overwhelming and His plan is bigger than you!

> *"…and to know this love that surpasses knowledge - that you may be filled to the measure of all the fullness of God. Now to Him who is able to do immeasurably more than all we ask or imagine, according to His power that is at work within us, to Him be glory in the church and in Christ Jesus throughout all generations, for ever and ever! Amen."*
> Ephesians 3:19-21

This segment is interesting because here is where I find myself closest to my ministry gift. When people see me, they often ask if I am a preacher or evangelist. I tell them that I am not. They look at me perplexed. I used to question God and ask, *"Why am I asked that question so much?"* Then I realized it's because I spend time with the Lord regularly. His countenance is all over me. Even when I experienced the lowest point in my life, I still spent time with the Lord. I realize I cannot survive without His presence. People can sense His aroma on me and the scent is *attractive*. My time with the Lord is where my strategies are developed, my vision is clarified, and my hope and faith are built.

My *Pain to Passion Workshop* started as a dream. I woke up and wrote it down. During my prayer time, God gave me instruction on how to make it come to pass. That is just **one** example of His ability to outpour.

God's Word says:

> *"I am the vine; you are the branches. If you remain in me and I in you, you will bear much fruit; apart from me you can do nothing. If you do not remain in me, you are like a branch that is thrown away and withers; such branches are picked up, thrown into the fire and burned. If you remain in me and my words remain in you, ask whatever you wish, and it will be done for you. This is to my Father's glory, that you bear much fruit, showing yourselves to be my disciples."*
> *(John 15:5-8).*

Take the time to get to know God and, in turn, you will get to know more and more about who **you** are. He knows every area of your life. You can share with Him your most intimate secrets. This is a time for cleansing and renewal. If there is anything you need to adjust, take the time to forgive yourself and ask God to show you how to move forward. There is no condemnation here. There is no shame here. There is no guilt - because in God's presence, judgement is absent. Allow His love to penetrate your heart.

Reflect, Rest, and Breathe

Remember that life is a journey and a process. Take the time in the presence of God to reflect on your accomplishments and your shortcomings. If you need to cry, then shed a tear. If you want to rejoice, then sing His praises. The key is to take a deep breath. As women, we have a lot of demands placed on us today. There are countless reasons why you should be overwhelmed with being busy...but ask yourself this question: *Is my "busyness" producing the outcome I expect to see?* Sometimes, the answer will be 'yes' for everyone else around you - but a resounding 'NO' for you.

You have to be honest with yourself. This is the time to look back at your **PAIN** and assess your path. Compare that with your passion and how you are progressing towards the goals. Don't get discouraged. Give yourself permission to rest. Then, prepare for the new day.

My sons play basketball and are (needless to say) huge fans of the game. As we watched a game on TV recently, I noticed the star players on both teams were pulled out during certain periods. I shouted at the TV, ***"Why did they take LeBron out?"*** My son would patiently explain: "Mom, because he has to rest before the 4th quarter." I again shouted, ***"But they are losing!"*** He then said, "Mom, they have plenty of time left in the game. It will be okay." Then it dawned on me: We, too, need rest. At any point in time, it seemed like I needed eight arms to get everything done that needed to get done...but more appendages were not the answers to my problems. I needed time to rest, refuel, grab a drink of water, and go back into the game harder than ever.

The Word of the Lord says, *"Come to me, all you who are weary and burdened, and I will give you rest. Take my yoke upon you and learn from me, for I am gentle and humble in heart, and you will find rest for your souls"* Matthew 11:27-29.

Take care of your physical body

Go hard or go home! I pride myself in operating in excellence - which is easier said than done. In my younger years, it seemed that I could run on fumes and do my best work under pressure. As I grew older, I realized my ship was slowing down.

It's funny how I took simple things for granted like being able to jump rope or sit Indian-style on the floor with no problem. There's an old adage: "If I knew then what I know now…" Well, if I **had** known, I would have been and done much better. I encourage you to take my advice and make adjustments to fuel your body so that you can sustain a healthy lifestyle. Get rid of anything and everything that is toxic in your life.

> *"Therefore, since we are surrounded by such a great cloud of witnesses, let us throw off everything that hinders and the sin that so easily entangles. And let us run with perseverance the race marked out for us, fixing our eyes on Jesus, the pioneer and perfecter of faith. For the joy set before Him, He endured the cross, scorning its shame, and sat down at the right hand of the throne of God. Consider Him who endured such opposition from sinners, so that you will not grow weary and lose heart."*
>
> Hebrews 12:1-3

There are a variety of ways to take care of your body: self-help books, videos, personal trainers, and fitness centers (just to name a few). You name it, the resources are out there. I am not suggesting you go out and take on some crazy challenge and set yourself up for failure. 'Taking care of your body' simply means this: Ask God, *"What do I need, Lord, in order to be able to sustain the vision you have given to me?"* The answer will be specific to **you**.

Be willing to adjust what you put into your body. After all, it will determine what comes out. Commit to sleep so that your body can regenerate cells. Craft **some** type of routine that will get your body in motion and alignment with God.

For years, I felt exhausted throughout the day until it finally got to the point where the doctor told me I had almost reached Chronic Fatigue, which required her to prescribe medication. **That** was a wakeup call for me. I became stressed because I had allowed the demands of my family, job, and business to wear me down. However, as I talked with my doctor and she ran tests, I found out I was anemic. My body was *extremely* deficient of iron due to blood loss. I had been that way since I was a teenager and never thought anything of it. In my 40s, that was a different story.

My first health goal was to work through the treatment plan and to consume more water. I had a 6-month and 12-month checkup that I needed to pass. I took anemia and my regimen to the Lord in prayer – and He healed me by changing my mindset. *"Do not conform to the pattern of this world, but be **transformed** by the renewing of your mind. Then you will be able to test and approve what God's will is - His good, pleasing, and perfect will."*(emphasis added) Romans 2:2. I had to become diligent about what I ate and consistent with my physical activity. As a result, I passed my 6-month **and**

12-month checkups! I still have to maintain a healthy lifestyle, but the **chronic** condition is no longer a factor despite my heavy demands, busy schedule, and stressors.

Commit to love yourself and determine practical ways to cope

The small adjustments I was willing to make on a regular basis made a difference in my quality of life. I could very well be on some type of medication that has multiple side-effects. However, I chose to commit to improving my inner-self by spending time with God regularly and improve my outer-self by taking care of my body. I'll be honest: As you read this book, I may not be at my goal *yet* - **BUT** I am better than where I started! I will continue to find ways to make little adjustments to improve. Living my passion requires a lot of energy, focus, and stamina.

There was a time in my life when I could not stand to see my own reflection. Every time I saw myself, I would break down in tears. The weight of the world was on my shoulders and I was broken. I was broken from my pitfalls in life: domestic violence and abuse, bad choices, guilt, shame, and just not knowing what to do next. There were a couple of rock-bottoms in my life as well. I went to counseling to get help - and that worked for a while, but drudging up my deepest pain was not healed through the counselor. I journaled, spoke positive, and even made vison board. It was not until I cried out to **God** to forgive and help me that my life shifted. It was a cry from deep down within the very core of my belly. His message back to me was to forgive and love myself.

Look, I know this book *may* be different than what you expected. Perhaps I am too raw with what I have experienced in life. Be mindful: My name Nikki – and that means "Victory of the people". I **had** to go through a lot of *PAIN* to get to the victory - which is my *PASSION*.

The profile of the woman in pain from Chapter One is my life on the surface. The Lord has allowed me to make it through a life of adversity so that **you** can expose **your** pain without guilt, shame, or fear. It does not matter what you have done, what has happened, or what you have allowed in your life up until now. *You can be free!* You don't have to write it in a book. No one has to know but you and God - but I encourage you to release it **ALL** to Him today!

Right now, pause and pray this **Prayer of Release from Pain** out loud:

*Father God, in the name of Jesus: I thank you for your Word that has given me a new **LIFE**.*

*I recognize you as my Lord and Savior and repent for the words, thoughts, actions, and deeds that were not like you. I denounce the **PAIN** of bondage that has kept me defeated and I receive you as LORD in every area of my life.*

Your Word says in Matthew 18:18 that whatsoever is bound in Earth shall be bound in Heaven and whatsoever is loosed in earth shall be loosed in Heaven.

*Therefore, in the name of Jesus - I bind my **PAIN** back to the pit of Hell from where it came, in Jesus' Name.*

*Now Father, I loose your unconditional love over my life and pray that the **JOY** of the LORD will overtake me right now.*

*Create in me a clean heart, O Lord, that I might serve **YOU** with boldness.*

I declare that I will demonstrate the fruit of your Spirit and walk upright before you.

*I **AM** the righteousness of GOD.*

*Thank you, Father, for allowing me to see that I am already more than a conqueror over my **PAIN**. Thank you for hearing my cry. Thank you for prayers that have already been answered in Jesus' Name.*

*Your Word says in Proverbs 18:10 that the Word of the Lord is a strong tower; the righteous run into it and they are safe. I declare today that **I AM SAFE** in your bosom - free to walk in the manifestation of the purpose that you predestined for me.*

*I no longer identify my **PAIN** as **WHO** I am, but rather see myself as **YOU** see me. I will walk in the manifestation of what you have **ALREADY DONE!***

*I **AM** a child of the **MOST** High God.*

*I **AM** victorious.*

*I **AM** free.*

*I **AM** a solution to unsolved problems in the Earth.*

*I **AM** a light in dark places.*

*I **AM** anointed to prosper.*

*I **AM** uniquely and wonderfully made. in Jesus' Name! Amen.*

Now it's time to prepare yourself for the marathon and live your passion. **Let the games begin!**

NOTES

_____

_____

_____

_____

_____

_____

_____

_____

_____

_____

_____

_____

_____

_____

_____

_____

_____

_____

No WeaPAIN Shall Prosper–CHEREE

Chapter 4
PLAN YOUR COURSE

You have just released your **PAIN** to God. The beauty of the release is that you are now positioned for God to deliver you from your pain. When you exposed the people, attitudes, insecurities, and negative perceptions that were getting in your way and gave it over to Christ, you made Him bigger than **any** situation or circumstance. That release freed you to focus on the thing God has purposed for you to do with your life. Some people refer to it as your "calling". Others call it "purpose" or "destiny". Whatever your vernacular or term used to describe your passion, God gave it to **you**. The question remains, *"How do I walk it out?"* There are things you can do to prepare you for the journey and undergird you with ways to combat the distractions that come your way.

*Why would **more** distractions come now that I am free, you ask?* As soon as you make the quality decision to expose your pain, live your passion, and release your will (purpose/passion) to Christ, the attacks will begin. It is time to act upon those commitments or fall back. James 1:23-25 reminds us, *"Don't fool yourself into thinking that you are a listener when you are anything but, letting the Word go in one ear and out the other. Act on what you hear! Those who hear and don't act are like those who glance in the mirror, walk away, and two minutes later have no idea who they are, what they look like. But whoever catches a glimpse of the revealed counsel of God - the free life! -even out of the corner of his eye, and sticks with it, is no distracted scatterbrain but a* *man or woman of action. That person will find delight and affirmation in the action"* (MSG).

Stay focused – for as you move into areas of passion, there is another level of pain that you must be prepared to handle. Although we like to blame everything on external factors or the devil, the following comes from within *you*: procrastination, abdicating your responsibility, internalizing fear, and not recognizing God for who He **really** is. I know that may seem overwhelming, but God **can** overcome your adversaries. *"When the enemy shall come in like a flood, the Spirit of the LORD shall lift up a standard against him"* (KJV). You have just made the **quality** decision to elevate your life and raise your standard. *That's* why it's important to know how to overcome the next level of pain and not allow yourself to be defeated.

Procrastination

Taking that first step towards living your passion is always the toughest. Procrastination will cause you to delay and allow people, attitudes, insecurities, and negative perceptions to reclaim their footholds in your life. You must have a plan of action or a course established for you to follow. This regimen will allow you to focus on what's ahead of you and never look back. As you begin to walk out your passion, you will realize that God *will* be with you.

> *"…for we walk by faith, not by sight - living
> our lives in a manner consistent with our
> confident belief in God's promises…"*
> 2 Corinthians 5:7 AMP

This book should become a call-to-action in your life. You did not pick this up by happenstance. Recognize the tug and pull - and respond **immediately** by asking God for direction.

> *"Ask and keep on asking and it will be
> given to you; seek and keep on seeking and
> you will find; knock and keep on knocking
> and the door will be opened to you."*
> Matthew 7:7 AMP

Others' lives are waiting on you to provide a solution to their problem. **Someone's** life is *literally* depending on you. When I reflect back on my journey, I wonder how many more lives I could have impacted had I written this book in 2010 when I first started writing the manuscript? I probably wandered around in my misery waiting for God to perform a miracle versus following His instruction to take one step forward in spite of my pain.

Abdicating Your Responsibility

When you take action in spite of your pain, God can then perform the work in you. ***However,*** we are required to do some work. So many of us are waiting on God to perform a miracle versus us doing our part. That is the abdication [refusal] to do what's within our control and handing it over to someone else - in this case, God — expecting Him to "fix it" for you. We have transferred our responsibility onto Him versus taking ownership. God has given you a *choice*. Choose today to honor the commitment you laid out for yourself in the earlier chapters of this book. If you need to take a moment to pause and reflect, then do so now. When you honor God and take the step forward, He will cause the increase to flow in the necessary areas of your life. You must exercise your faith and do something! *"Wasn't our ancestor Abraham "made right with God by works" when he placed his son Isaac on the sacrificial altar? Isn't it obvious that faith and works are yoked partners, that faith expresses itself in works? That the works are "works of faith"? The full meaning of "believe" in the Scripture sentence, "Abraham believed God and was set right with God," includes his action. It's that mesh of believing and acting that got Abraham named "God's friend." Is it not evident that a person is made right with God not by a barren faith but by faith fruitful in works?"* (MSG).

I can remember asking God, *"Why didn't you just give me the download of this book in a dream like you did the workshops?"* What I came to realize is that the book required even **more** study, **more** painful experiences with which to draw from, and **more** time in His presence. I had to seek Him like never before and draw closer to Him to truly gain wisdom. It's one thing to share knowledge with others, but *wisdom keys* are crucial to breaking bondages and chains in others. This is my second pass at writing this book. Hopefully, you will see that God was waiting on me...and not me waiting on Him.

Internalizing Fear

What was I afraid of? The grip of fear to pursue your passion can be paralyzing. At every workshop I conducted, **everyone** could recite the acronym for **FEAR: F**alse **E**vidence **A**ppearing **R**eal - but what does it **really** mean? Whoever penned that acronym hit the nail right on the head. When we take on fear to the point where we allow the *illusion* of what can happen in the worst possible way to overshadow the passions God has given to us, **then** we begin the pain cycle all over again. As I thought about my own fears, I realized I had both a fear of failure **and** a fear of success.

Until my early adult life, I was a people-pleaser. I never wanted to let anyone down and was afraid that if I did not go to college, get a good job, get married, and have children, I would be a failure in everyone's eyes. Despite striving to meet those expectations, I had a lot of missteps along the way. My accomplishments always seemed to have a *'BUT'* attached to it. Sure I went to college, *but* I graduated with a child, husband, and a dysfunctional marriage. My first career job was at a Fortune 500 company, *but* it was an entry-level customer service position. A few of my extended family members mocked me because by that time, I had two children and a **very** low salary (even though I had a

Master's Degree). I felt like I was a shame and embarrassment to them.

On the flip side, as I grew in my faith and walked with the Lord, I became more and more successful. God allowed me to overcome my adversity, but I still felt the sting of the same type of fear grip me. The difference then was that I was afraid of becoming **too** successful and having my family and friends saying, "Don't forget where you came from! Who do you think you are? You think you are "all that" in that position!" ***BUT God!*** He transformed me by the renewing of my mind and let me know:

"For God hath not given us the spirit of fear;
but of power, and of love, and of a sound mind."
(emphasis added)
2 Timothy 1:7 KJV

Not Recognizing God for Who He Really Is

We see all types of award shows on television today. There is a designated time when the entertainment industries recognize or give honor to others' achievements. During the acceptance speeches, the winners will give honor to those who helped support them along the way. May I say that my **first** exhortation belongs to Christ?

There was a period of awakening in my life when I needed to truly know that God was real. People described Him as 'something bigger than themselves' or a 'higher power'. I know God to be the Father, Son, and Holy Ghost. Jesus Christ is my Lord and Savior. Without Him, I am *nothing*. He is Jehovah Jireh - my Provider. He is Jehovah Shalom - my Peace. He is my Comforter. He is my Confidant and Trusted Advisor. He is my Shelter when everything around me is bleak. He is the Air that I breathe. He is my Resting Place. He is Strength and fights for me when I am weak. He is the Lamp unto my feet and the Light unto my path. He is the Creative Force that brings my dreams to fruition. He is The One who makes a way for me out of no way. He is my Healer when I am sick. He is the Light at the end of the tunnel. He is my very Best Friend; on Him I can depend. Belief in Him allows me to believe in myself – who He created me to be in the Earth. I can look back over my life at all of the times I was in a bad situation, alone, and afraid. I now know I was *never* alone; He was *always* there with me.

I want you to spend some time right now to truly recognize just who God is in your life. After all, He will provide you the way of escape and deliver you from your pain.

> *"And whoever shall call on the name of the Lord shall be delivered and saved, for in Mount Zion and in Jerusalem there shall be those who escape, as the Lord has said, and among the remnant [of survivors] shall be those whom the Lord calls."*
>
> Joel 2:32 AMP

NOTES

_____

_____

_____

_____

_____

_____

_____

_____

_____

_____

_____

_____

_____

_____

_____

_____

_____

_____

_____

_____

_____

No WeaPAIN Shall Prosper–CHEREE

Chapter 5
VISION PLAN

Step 1

N ow, let's remain focused on the choice **you** made to move forward with your passion. Together, let's look at three practical steps we can do that will allow us to progress forward as we rely and depend on God to enable us to fulfill our passion:

This step will help you understand how to answer **PAIN**-ful questions such as: *Is it God, me, or the devil? Where is my life headed? Where do I see myself? If I know what my passion is, how do I see it, touch it, or get it all over me?* In order to answer these questions, you must have a vision for your life. Let's compare the importance of vision from modern dictionary versus biblical terms:

The *modern [online] dictionary* defines vision as:

1) The act or power of sensing with the eyes; sight. 2) The act or power of anticipating that which will or may come to be: prophetic vision; the vision of an entrepreneur. 3) An experience in which a personage, thing, or event appears vividly or credibly to the mind, although not actually present, often under the influence of a divine or other agency: a heavenly messenger appearing in a vision. 4) Something seen or otherwise perceived during such an experience. 5) A vivid, imaginative conception or anticipation: visions of wealth and glory.

What the *Holy Bible* says about vision:

> *"Write the vision, and make it plain upon tables, that he may run that readeth it."*
>
> Habakkuk 2:2-3

"Where there is no vision, the people perish…"
Proverbs 29:18

"Order my steps in thy word: and let not any iniquity have dominion over me."
Psalm 119:133

"For whatsoever things were written aforetime were written for our learning, that we through patience and comfort of the scriptures might have hope."
Romans 15:4

Each biblical description demonstrates the importance of looking beyond the present and seeing something bigger ahead. There is a divine aspect that leads the person with a vision into a broader, larger landscape - and preparation (i.e. writing it down) is a key element. As we write our visions down, God orders our steps and has dominion over us. When we look back and reflect on them, we will see that we have expanded and increased as we follow Christ. Our visions are connected to our passion and detached from pain.

When you talk about your passion, can you **see** it? Can you **sense** it? As long as you are advancing forward (taking necessary steps), it *will* come to pass. Your vision will evolve as you mature in the things of God. You will be able to focus with your foresight because you know what He has already delivered you from. Stand - like Abraham - on the promises of God:

> *"This is why the fulfillment of God's promise depends entirely on trusting God and His way, and then simply embracing Him and what He does. God's promise arrives as a pure gift. That's the only way everyone can be sure to get in on it, those who keep the religious traditions and those who have never heard of them. For Abraham is father of us all. He is not our racial father—that's reading the story backward. He is our faith father. We call Abraham "father" not because he got God's attention by living like a saint, but because God made something out of Abraham when he was a nobody. Isn't that what we've always read in Scripture, God saying to Abraham, "I set you up as father of many peoples"? Abraham was first named "father" and then became a father because he dared to trust God to do what only God could do: raise the dead to life, with a word make something out of nothing. When everything was hopeless, Abraham believed anyway, deciding to live not on the basis of what he saw he couldn't do but on what God said he would do. And so he was made father of a multitude of peoples. God Himself said to him, "You're going to have a big family, Abraham!"*
> (Romans 4:16-18 MSG)

By faith, the pain you thought was a big deal will become smaller...and God will become bigger and bigger on the inside of us. As He expands **in** you, He can outpour **through** you – and you can get to the next level. Then, it duplicates your efforts through others.

As I pondered over the word vision, God showed me that He has granted me **V.I.S.I.O.N.** – **V**isual **I**nsight of **S**uccess **I**n spite of **O**pposition **N**ow! I took those wisdom keys and formulated my vision ... one that would allow me to execute my *passion*. We know that where we are today is not where He will have us to be in the end.

Visual

The visual aspect of your vision is likened to having a mountain top view or perspective. Imagine yourself looking down on a beautiful scene where you can see a wide range of landscape. That's the perspective you should have for your vision; a big, broad view of just how far your passion can take you. Be ambitious! Don't allow pain to hold you in the box. The bigger your vision, the better. You should not focus from a bottom (or valley) point of view because you can become easily overwhelmed by everything all around you. Allow yourself to use the faith "lenses" God has given you: The ability to see beyond what we can think or perceive in our present situation. A familiar and relatable analogy is 'soaring like an eagle'. When eagles search for prey, they can soar high above the ground and see the entire playing field below. They are then able to strategically strike the critical place to obtain their food; their life-sustaining sustenance. **Believe** that your vision can and will come to pass. Have faith in your vision. Write it down.

Insight of

When you document your vision you will receive insight that is inspired by the Father, discerned through the Holy Spirit, and conceived in prayer. The process may take time and will evolve through the intimacy of knowing God for yourself. *"…[looking away from all that will distract us and] focusing our eyes on Jesus, who is the Author and Perfecter of faith [the first incentive for our belief and the One who brings our faith to maturity], who for the joy [of accomplishing the goal] set before Him endured the cross, disregarding the shame, and sat down at the right hand of the throne of God [revealing His deity, His authority, and the completion of His work]"* (Hebrews 12:2 AMP). That means you do not have to spend a lot of time wondering about how you're going to do it. Spend time focusing on **BEING YOU** while taking steps to master the good thing you are most passionate about.

Success

Your success should be defined by you and no one else. Do not be or become a people-pleaser *(as I, admittedly, once was)*. That's not God's desire for you. Your goal should be to please **Him**. No matter how small or large your contribution, there should be no limit to what you can achieve. Remember: God has given you gifts – talents which fuel your passion – for a reason. Your dedication, hard work, and determination are the legwork and His anointing provides the increase for you to live a life of passion. Don't worry about whether you have enough resources, time, etc. *"If God gives such attention to the appearance of wildflowers - most of which are never even seen - don't you think He'll attend to you, take pride in you, do His best for you? What I'm trying to do here is to get you to relax, to not be so preoccupied with getting, so you can respond to God's giving. People who don't know God and the way he works fuss over these things, but you know both God and how he works. Steep your life in God-reality, God-initiative, God-provisions. Don't worry about missing out. You'll find all your everyday human concerns will be met"* (Matthew 6:33 MSG). As you bless others through your passion, He will bless you to grow!

In spite of

It doesn't matter what it looks like! *"For though we live in the world, we do not wage war as the world does. The weapons we fight with are not the weapons of the world. On the contrary, they have divine power to demolish strongholds. We demolish arguments and every pretension that sets itself up against the knowledge of God, and we take captive every thought to make it obedient to Christ"* (2 Corinthians 10:3-5). When you realize that you belong to Christ, you will come to recognize His favor, grace, and mercy. Continue to press through struggles, denounce pain, and focus on the bigger picture. If you have made it to this point and are still reading this book, look at how far you have come! This is the first step. In spite of every level of pain, there is **hope**.

> *"Be strong and courageous. Do not be afraid or terrified because of them, for the LORD your God goes with you; He will never leave you nor forsake you."*
> Dueteronomy31:6

Opposition

Many great men and women who have become the best athlete, musician, congressman, or businessperson failed several times before they reached their goal. Sometimes, the roadblocks and pitfalls seemed unsurmountable. Many doors were closed. The expectation is not that you will never face opposition, but the key is to never **quit**. *"And that about wraps it up. God is strong, and he wants you strong. So take everything the Master has set out for you, well-made weapons of the best materials. And put them to use so you will be able to stand up to everything the devil throws your way. This is no afternoon athletic contest that we'll walk away from and forget about in a couple of hours. This is for keeps, a life-or-death fight to the finish against the devil and all his angels. Be prepared. You're up against far more than you can handle on your own. Take all the help you can get, every weapon God has issued, so that when it's all over but the shouting you'll still be on your feet. Truth, righteousness, peace, faith, and salvation are more than words. Learn how to apply them. You'll need them throughout your life. God's Word is an indispensable weapon. In the same way, prayer is essential in this ongoing warfare. Pray hard and long. Pray for your brothers and sisters. Keep your eyes open. Keep each other's spirits up so that no one falls behind or drops out"* (Ephesians 6:12-18 MSG). Know that if anyone other than you could have done what you do better, it would already be done. God has a plan for you. He needs for you to deliver 'it' to the world against all odds.

Now!

This is a call-to-action! In this very moment, you are exercising your faith to act by reading this book and following through on the steps it outlines. No one knows your heart but you and God. However, I **know** what it feels like to be hurt and in despair. When I was picking up trash in order to have money deducted from my rent, I told the Lord that is not where I wanted to end up. I had to **do** something. I kept picking up trash and focusing on my goals until one day, things turned around for the better. I encourage you to stand for what you believe in - and that is **YOU**. You *are* enough and a *gift* to this world. Don't wait for anyone to do it for you…make the decision to write down and act upon your vision - **now**!

A common approach to documenting your vision is to create a Passion Board. It typically takes 45 minutes to an hour to create an 8" x 10" board. Use materials such as words, pictures, and symbols that refer to where you see yourself in both the short- and long-term. Once your board has been created, post it in an accessible location. Examine it daily as an encouragement to you. It will represent the tangible evidence of what you can't see now. Remember to speak positively over your passion and do not share or allow any negative people to know your thoughts. Finally, measure your progress by placing stars (or any form of reward or recognition) on any area you have completed on your board. *If you need ideas, the Internet is a great place to search.*

NOTES

Chapter 6
PREPARE, PRACTICE, PRINCIPLES

Step 2

This step will help you understand how to answer **PAIN**-ful questions such as: *What is my focus? How do I get started? Can I stay on track? God, when are you going to fix this for me?* We all start out with good intentions. You may see results for a few weeks and feel like you are gaining momentum. Then, at some point, you may lose steam and allow the distractions of life to take your eyes off of the passion.

I know that over time, I have failed miserably at completing my New Year's resolutions to lose weight or exercise more. My longest-standing track record was three full weeks of rigorous activity - then I fell off the cliff, never to return. My hopes of the perfect physique succumbed to Oreo cookies and milk...or salt and vinegar chips. What I found is that my next attempt to get back into the swing of things would be even harder, so I had to become more strategic in my approach and tackle my goals in a way that would build consistency and stamina.

There were three critical areas of focus I found to create improvement in my life. I had to: 1. Prepare my mind; 2. Plan my day; and 3. Promote my vision.

Prepare Your Mind

A part of my preparation started with changing my mindset. By now, you may have noticed the consistent theme that has worked for me; beginning everything by trusting God. A part of changing my mind meant changing my sight or what I could see around me. The *environment* around me had not been conducive to living a pain-free life. My road to passion has not been easy (to say the least), but I refuse to doubt why God placed me on this Earth.

I can remember a very painful experience that has stuck with me for a long time - one where I learned a very valuable lesson. As a teenager, I had the knack for choosing the wrong guy to date. There I was on a full scholarship to The Ohio State University - and I was dating a drug dealer. All of his friends were either dealers or users, and I was in the midst of them…standing out like a sore thumb. One day, my boyfriend and I got into a vicious argument, and I was struggling with the choice of whether or not to remain in the relationship. *Everything* inside of me was telling me to **get out** - although he desperately wanted me to stay. The argument climaxed when he pulled out a gun and pointed it at my head. He told me that if he could not have me, then no one could. I mustered up the courage to tell him to just shoot me. I was so angry. I was willing to lose my life in order to feel like I was in control. Due to my sexual abuse at a young age, I had vowed to myself to never give a man power over me to take what belonged to me. Looking back, I thank God for grace because in all actuality, I had no control of that situation and was at my boyfriend's mercy. Fortunately, my behavior startled my now-ex-boyfriend. He put the gun down, wrote me off as "crazy", apologized, and admitted the gun was not loaded.

I was able to get out of that relationship, live another day, and never see him again. Still, **something** had to change. *What was I doing wrong?* I did not speak faith in that situation, but chose to allow the words of self-destruction to come out of my mouth. I knew that I had to change. All of the positive things I was doing at the time were being drowned out by poor choices and a dangerous lifestyle. I had to change my *words* because they framed how I saw myself. As well, the people around me were feeding me death - not life. I had to eliminate naysayers and bad influences. The atmosphere was toxic and affected my mindset.

As I have matured, I learned to surrender my will and allow **God** to lead me. Like me, God has invited *you* to more than enough. I encourage you to accept the invitation that He has given you to live pain-free. Although it may be hard at first, I encourage you to look back and take the opportunity to self-reflect - to review your accomplishments, mistakes, and the experiences you have made it through. Don't worry about the "bad stuff": We all have rough patches. See your mistakes not as the end, but rather the start of something new. Then, work every single day to create a new environment.

Plan Your Day

As you begin each day, remain in the frame of mind that God is your *First Priority*. Then, create a consistent *Routine* in place of 'busy' work or activities that don't feed into you realizing your passion. I know that things will come up that are outside of your control, so be willing to stay flexible. During your cycle of prayer and reflection, you will learn how to adjust your plans as needed. A consistent routine will require you to *Take Deliberate Action*. You will not become successful by accident. Preparation works and is a fundamental key to sustaining your success. Sustaining takes effort, so walk in *Peace*. There will be times when you get discouraged or move from a mountain view to a valley view, but remember: You have power. *"Jesus answered and said unto them, Verily I say unto you, If ye have faith, and doubt not, ye shall not only do this which is done to the fig tree, but also if ye shall say unto this mountain, Be thou removed, and be thou cast into the sea; it shall be done"* (Matthew 21:21 KJV). No one can control your destiny – and God is with you.

Next, track *Your Progress*. I have three children. With each child, I took them to the doctor where they would measure weight, height, etc. That information would let the doctor know if my child was healthy and progressing at an age-appropriate rate. ***Why wouldn't we do that with our dreams and aspirations?*** You should take the time to celebrate small wins along the way and see yourself develop a pattern of victory! Make adjustments for areas of opportunity. You will soon begin to recognize the promises of God have come to pass in your life.

There are various tools and resources available to you to map out your goals on a daily basis. The key is to start with what you have. A few common examples are: a planner, budget worksheet, journal, Smart Phone, business plan, and, of course, the Word of God! Use them to create a 30/60/90-day plan of attack.

In the first 30 days, you will assess what needs to be accomplished. Seek God and *Identify Required Resources*, tools, and finances you need to obtain your goal. This is also a great time to replace the haters, takers, fakers, and waiters and *Get to Know People* who can build you up and support your vision (i.e. Mentors) or the best option of all...begin to spend more time with the most important person - your **SAVIOR**!

During the second phase (days 31- 60), you should develop a high-level plan and maintain a *Solution Mindset*. Use your passion board as a guide. Although you may not have all of the finite details, you **will** have an understanding of where you are headed and what the end goal should be. Commit the plan to writing by drafting it out on paper. *Assume Accountability* for your actions. Here, you may want to identify someone whom you can trust to hold you accountable to meet those goals. One person will suffice. Be prayerful and discern the fakers and takers who are not completely out of your life by this point.

The final 30 days (days 61-90), you should be implementing your plan. ***Now*** you can begin to communicate what you are working on, as you may need people to assist you. Ask God to give you wisdom on what to *Communicate*. Then, take *Action* and make *Adjustments* by further refining the details that are within your control on a daily, weekly, and monthly basis.

The fundamental aspect of the 30/60/90-day plan of attack is to be honest with yourself. Don't begrudge baby steps. Let go of excuses! Keep it simple and work the 90-day cycle. Only commit to a powerful few by identifying the top three things you can commit to completing within the first 30, 60, and then 90-day intervals. Those big buckets will require several activities related to it that need to get accomplished that you can break down even further. Plot them on your planner (or whatever tool you use to track progress). Share them with your *Accountability Partner.*

Promote Your Vision

As your pattern of victory begins to materialize, you will begin to expand. This means that your vision - your foresight - will become fine-tuned and you will *Recognize Opportunities* that can accelerate your growth. This is no small feat, so you must be willing to assume the *Stretch Position*. Expansion can be a painful process as you go beyond your own skill and ability. Do not be afraid! Lean into the *Discomfort* and allow God to promote you.

I can remember when I took my first job as a manager leading people in a plant. I did not think anyone would take me seriously because I looked young. So, I went to work with my hair pinned up in a bun. To me, that made me look older and credible. What I did not realize is that it was not the look my team needed. They needed to know that I was able to perform the job. They teased me and would ask why such a young woman would wear her hair back in a bun. Finally, I got the point.

I had to take the opportunity to *Be Courageous*! Yes, this was my first time leading people in a male-dominated industry with a team of employees in which most of them were older than me, but I was equipped and ready to take on the role. I challenged myself to demonstrate what I could do - which enabled them to have trust and confidence in me. I performed my job with excellence and supported each of them as they accomplished their own objectives. Word begin to spread about our team's achievements. As I networked in the organization, when someone asked me about myself, I was armed with my "elevator speech".

*An **elevator speech** is a short summary used to quickly and simply define a product, service, or organization and its value proposition.* The term "elevator speech" is indicative of the idea that it should be possible to deliver a summary in the timespan of an elevator ride - approximately 30 seconds to no more than two minutes.

I encourage you to prepare your elevator speech to *Who You Are, What Problem You Solve, What Need You Fulfill,* and the *Notable Impact.* People will begin to seek you out simply for the passion that rests within you.

Below is an acronym that has helped guide me on how to demonstrate my ability with **G.O.D.L.Y.** conduct:

G

Give your best. (Acts 11:29): *Then the disciples, every man according to his ability, determined to send relief unto the brethren which dwelt in Judaea.*

Go the extra mile. (Philippians 3:14): *I press toward the mark for the prize of the high calling of God in Christ Jesus.*

Gain wisdom, knowledge, and understanding in your area. (Proverbs 4:7): *Wisdom is the principal thing; therefore, get wisdom: and with all thy getting get understanding.*

O

Operate with a Spirit of Excellence. (Galatians 5:22-23): *But the fruit of the Spirit is love, joy, peace, longsuffering, gentleness, goodness, faith, Meekness, temperance: against such there is no law.*

Open your heart to be led by the Holy Spirit. (Psalm 37:23): *The steps of a good man are ordered by the LORD: and he delighteth in his way.*

Obey God's Word and follow His instruction. (I John 3:24): *And he that keepeth his commandments dwelleth in him, and he in him. And hereby we know that he abideth in us, by the Spirit which he hath given us.*

D

Demonstrate professionalism and integrity. (2 Timothy 2:15): *Study to shew thyself approved unto God, a workman that needeth not to be ashamed, rightly dividing the word of truth.*

Discipline yourself in diligence and consistency. (1 Corinthians 9:24-27): *Know ye not that they* which run in a race run all, but one receiveth the prize? So run, that ye may obtain. And every man that striveth for the mastery is temperate in all things. Now they do it to obtain a corruptible crown; but we an incorruptible. I therefore so run, not as uncertainly; so fight I, not as one that beateth the air; But I keep under my body, and bring it into subjection: lest that by any means, when I have preached to others, I myself should be a castaway.

Determine that God is the source of your supply. (1 Timothy 6:17): *Charge them that are rich in this world, that they be not high-minded, nor trust in uncertain riches, but in the living God, who giveth us richly all things to enjoy;*

L

Let your lifestyle speak for you. (Romans 12:1-3): *I beseech you therefore, brethren, by the mercies of God, that ye present your bodies a living sacrifice, holy, acceptable unto God, which is your reasonable service. And be not conformed to this world: but be ye transformed by the renewing of your mind, that ye may prove what is that good, and acceptable, and perfect, will of God. For I say, through the grace given unto me, to every man that is among you, not to think of himself more highly than he ought to think; but to think soberly, according as God hath dealt to every man the measure of faith.*

Love what you do. (John 6:27): *Labour not for the meat which perisheth, but for that meat which endureth unto everlasting life, which the Son of man shall give unto you: for him hath God the Father sealed.*

Listen to God. (John 10:27): *My sheep hear my voice, and I know them, and they follow me.*

Y

You are your worst critic. (Romans 8:37): *Nay, in all these things we are more than conquerors through him that loved us.*

You are not alone. (Romans 8:38-39): *For I am persuaded, that neither death, nor life, nor angels, nor principalities, nor powers, nor things present, nor things to come, Nor height, nor depth, nor any other creature, shall be able to separate us from the love of God, which is in Christ Jesus our Lord.*

Your attitude determines your altitude. (Colossians 1:10): *That ye might walk worthy of the Lord unto all pleasing, being fruitful in every good work, and increasing in the knowledge of God.*

NOTES

No WeaPAIN Shall Prosper–CHEREE

Chapter 7
OVERCOME OBSTACLES

Step 3

This step will help you understand how to answer **PAIN**-ful questions such as: *God are you still there? What do I do now? What happens if I fail? How do I recover from setbacks? If He did it for you, can He do it for me? Who can I trust?* There will be a time during your process where you will have to take a stand and fight for what you believe in. *"Therefore, my beloved brothers and sisters, be steadfast, immovable, always excelling in the work of the Lord [always doing your best and doing more than is needed], being continually aware that your labor [even to the point of exhaustion] in the Lord is not futile nor wasted [it is never without purpose]. Having done all to stand"* (1 Corinthians 15:58 AMP). The pathway to passion can take twists and turns, but the outcome will remain with you.

There are so many ways you can look at how to overcome obstacles. Following are ways that have worked for me:

Be a pillar

Understanding your purpose comes with great responsibility. That means you may have to humble yourself and submit to someone else's vision before you can accomplish your own. This is often the most common obstacle that someone faces when they are on fire and realize their purpose. Being a *pillar* means that you are a strength, support, and help to someone else - despite your need. When you recognize the role that you may first play with someone else's vision, you can begin to glean what is required for you to reach *your* goal. You will develop mental fortitude, patience, and joy from positively impacting those around you. This may require **sacrifice** on your part by operating behind the scenes - *if* your nature is being a leader.

A part of overcoming obstacles is learning how to fight with skill. When you support someone else's dream, you see how they react and respond; you see what challenges they had to overcome, and you can relish in victory after bearing witness to what they have been through. I am **not** suggesting that in this phase as a pillar, you abandon your passion altogether. I **am** suggesting that you take the time to hone your skills, become educated, and learn the pros and cons. Build trust with others so they can help you anticipate the barriers that need to be removed and devise a plan to overcome them. Your time is coming!

> *"Wait on the LORD: be of good courage,*
> *and he shall strengthen thine heart: wait,*
> *I say, on the LORD."*
> Psalm27:14 KJV

Ask for help

Sometimes, you are not prepared for what life throws your way. ***Ask for help.*** I can remember vividly the screams of my children during a domestic violence situation when I was pinned down on the living room floor while being hit in the face by my now-ex-husband and nearly choked to the point of unconsciousness. At first, I could barely mouth the words, but I kept saying, ***"I will live and not die! I will live and not die!"*** At one point, I was screaming it out loud and my abuser's response was that Jesus couldn't help me – as my children watched on in terror. Oh, was **he** wrong! In what seemed like an instant, the doorbell rang. That window of opportunity for me was a distraction to him. As he went to answer the front door, I bolted out of the back door in my underwear, ran into the street, and ***screamed*** for someone to help me – and someone came to my rescue.

I used that example to say this: Your journey to live out your passion will not be done in isolation. Recognize that a part of your arsenal is knowing how to reach out for help when you need it. Ask the Lord to help you. Just as God uses you to help someone else achieve their goal, God will assign someone to your life. It may be only for a season, but He will provide. Remember that whatever the provision, God gave it to you. Honor Him by being a conduit and reciprocating the action in someone else's life.

Set realistic expectations and prepare

Your role is to be specific with what you ask for. Be responsible. Use the resources for what they are intended. Be grateful…and do not feel *entitled*. People will be drawn to you as they see the ***"blessings of God"*** manifest in your life. Mind you: Every gift is not from God. Remember the old adage, "Everything that glitters isn't gold"? Too many people lose everything by selling their souls for immediate reward or instant gratification. Your passion is not a get-rich-quick scheme, but a lifelong journey with deposits along the way.

Be prudent. Be patient. Much like the Stock Market, you will have up and down seasons. As you work your vision and draft your plans, make sure you take stock. Get your financial affairs in order.

> *"Suppose one of you wants to build a tower.*
> *Won't you first sit down and estimate the cost to*
> *see if you have enough money to complete it?*
> *For if you lay the foundation and are not able to*
> *finish it, everyone who sees it will ridicule you."*
> Luke 14:28-29

Take small steps to save and be realistic with your expectations. Every little bit counts. Be frugal and spend wisely. Store brand is just as good as name brand items in times of need. I can remember when I first discovered

Aldi discount grocery store. I was so excited about the amount of food I could get at a lower price. One of my coworkers laughed at me because I shopped there for my children's lunch. She could not understand why I did not shop at a more "upscale" chain. A few years and several children later, she came back to me as she faced difficult times and asked me what the name of the store was at which I shopped. By this time, I was at the point where I was able to supplement Aldi with other store chains, but I told her the name and never thought twice about it. Hard times will come; however, you have the ability to prepare for them in advance.

> *"Keep a cool head. Stay alert. The devil is poised to pounce, and would like nothing better than to catch you napping. Keep your guard up. You're not the only ones plunged into these hard times. It's the same with Christians all over the world. So keep a firm grip on the faith. The suffering won't last forever. It won't be long before this generous God who has great plans for us in Christ - eternal and glorious plans they are! - will have you put together and on your feet for good. He gets the last word; yes, He does."*
>
> 1 Peter 5:9-11 MSG

Just say No

You may wonder why I have "Just say no" here. There are three reasons:

1. As we flow in our gifts and passions, we can become overly-optimistic about what we can take on;

2. As pillars, we can take on too much for everyone else; and

3. You become dissatisfied with your progress.

It is important to note here that as you spend time with God, you must get into the habit of asking **Him** how to prioritize. Multitasking can be the death of your dream because you are spread too thin and not able to master anything.

Like many of you, I am a mother, wife, employee, daughter, sister, church member, etc. There are *many* demands placed on me. Part of my obstacle was being able to understand when I was overwhelmed - and how to say "No" to people and things. I have become more selective about when I accept an engagement, take on another project, and how much "help" I can provide. The ability to evaluate and assess what triggered stress in my life or put in me in positons to get distracted is a daily walk. I have gotten *much* better at saying "No". *This part will come with some resistance, but I encourage you to stay focused.*

You will need focus when you reach a plateau or a place where you feel like you are not moving fast enough. Just say "No!" to frustration, fear, and worry. Do not allow pain to creep back in and take root in your heart. Remember: Slow progress is still progress. There may be things that need to be moved out of your way so that you are prepared for the next level. There may be work in you *(pain)* that you need to be freed from so that you do not damage other people as you live out your passion. *"There is a season (a time appointed) for everything and a time for every delight and event or purpose under Heaven"* (Ecclesiastes 3:3 AMP). Reject the **lies** that say 'You will never amount to anything' or 'That is as high as you can go'. *Believe* in who you are.

NOTES

No WeaPAIN Shall Prosper–CHEREE

Chapter 8
LIVE PAIN-FREE

W alking out your passion is a choice. It's a quality decision that you must make every day, which takes the focus off of the *pain* that you may experience and replaces it with **PASSION**. Based on everything discussed thus far: You have learned that you are *already* equipped to win! Now, the question becomes: *"Once I reach a goal or milestone, then what do I do?"* The answer is simple. Just **BE**! "Do you" in the most transparent, humble, and fantastic way possible! You will leave a legacy behind for generations to come.

I think about my grandmother who recently passed away and how important she was to my family. She was born in Alabama, picked cotton growing up, moved North to find a better opportunity, and raised eight children. She found a job as a cook in the local hospital. That woman was the **best cook ever**! I can remember all of the cakes, pies, and dinners she made for everyone. Each dish was filled with love and tasted SO good! Her house was the center of our family for *at least* 50 years. If you ever needed to find anyone or know what was happening, just call or go see Ma Pope. Her phone number and address never changed – and she was willing to tell **all** of your business.

When Ma Pope died, all of the family and friends came in large numbers to pay tribute. My grandmother lived her passion and used her love of family and food to bring people together. We sat over the dinner table and talked about God, family, relationships, politics, etc. I cherish those moments and strive to create similar ones with my family and friends. No one can replace my grandmother, but the things she taught us about faith in God, love of family, and how to overcome hardships was passed on to and through each of us. My grandmother had a hard life, but she made the best out of every moment. She used every opportunity to share her stories and teach us how to be better - not to mention we all learned how to cook at least *one* of her famous dishes.

I have learned some valuable wisdom keys about how to live a pain-free life from Ma Pope.

It's not about you

It's easy to believe that all of the pain you go through is all about you. Oftentimes, when you experience pain, you feel like no one else can *possibly* understand. However, when I recall the story of Jesus' life, His was filled with disappointments and tragedy. Ultimately, Jesus died on the cross not for Himself, but for you and me. *"For God so loved the world that he gave his one and only Son, that whoever believes in him shall not perish but have eternal life"* (John 3:16). Like Christ, your suffering is not in vain. As you move from triumph to triumph, your role is to teach, develop, and mentor someone else so they can learn from you. You are never too young or too old to share your story.

God enabled me to navigate through Hell and back from a small child to an adult mother of three. As Marvin Sapp's song lyric states: *"I **never** would have made it without you [God]. I am stronger, wiser, better."* I take advantage of the opportunity to sow seeds like my grandmother did. The return cannot be measured. I have seen women who have spent time with me flourish and blossom. For that, I am truly grateful. It is an honor to serve someone else.

The *Pain to Passion* workshop is a vehicle to share some of the lessons I have learned along the way. It allows me to be free of the sting from ***pain*** I once endured – and I am optimistic that no one else has to walk in my shoes. If you are living similar experiences right now in this very moment, know that if I made it through, so can you. I know that I am a winner because I am on **God's** team. *Pain to Passion* launched in a small hotel room. There was no profit and no fanfare; just me with a desire to help women through difficult circumstances. I encourage you to use whatever platform you have available to invest in someone in the workplace, church, school, and/or home. One seed sown and nurtured **will** bear fruit and multiply.

Don't stop "there"

Once I've reached a certain goal, I believe I have reached the mountain top. I breathe a sigh of relief because the pinnacle of my success was achieved. Does that sound like you? I challenge you: Once you experience success in one area, **don't stop there**. That place called "there" – your definition of success – is not the end. Continue the process and God will continue to expand your territory and increase you. Remember: As you develop a pattern of victory, other doors will become available to you.

I think about my evolution through Corporate America. As I mentioned earlier in the book, my first career role was an Entry-Level Customer Service positon – despite having an advanced degree. Some of my family members were disappointed, but I was a freshly-divorced single mother with two children. I had to provide for them on my own. I lived in my grandmother's basement until I could obtain an apartment based on my income. However, because I had a job, I had to pay full rent because my income was not below the poverty line. I was caught between a rock and hard place, but resolved to climb the corporate ladder and make something out of my life.

The first couple of years on the job, I volunteered for additional assignments, took online courses, and went above and beyond to prove myself every chance I had.

My goal was to become a Training and Development Leader - which was a part of the Human Resources (HR) Department. Once the position opened up and was posted, I applied for it. I was turned down for not having enough HR experience. My degree was in Business Administration. In fact, I was turned down two more times for positions within the Training Department for one reason or another. I could not understand why I was being overlooked.

Sensing my discouragement, one of my mentors advised me to reach out to HR for help to understand what the positions required. My HR coach was a blessing from God. She worked with me to identify my top five strengths. We then began to look at every open position that matched my skills and qualifications in order to determine whether or not I should apply. After several months of no-go decisions, a positon within the Human Resources Development Program (HRDP) was posted. At this point, I still had no HR experience, but I **did** possess a *passion* for training. The HRDP was a rotational program that would allow me to learn various aspects of HR and determine where I could be most effective. I immediately applied.

My HR coach advised me to set up an 'Informational Interview' with the Hiring Manager to learn more about the program and to give him an opportunity to get to know me before a formal interview. The Hiring

Manager was the Vice President (VP) of HR. He agreed to meet with me based on the credibility of my coach, but he was very clear: Only external college graduates could apply. I persisted. I explained to him why it would be the right opportunity for me and showed him my resume (which included a Master's Degree in Business Administration). Again, he emphatically told me he was not looking for someone who was interested in HR and was not *qualified*. He instructed me to go talk to another HR Director, and if *he* said I was a viable candidate, I would then have a chance to interview for the positon.

Little did I know ... the HR Director he sent me to speak with was the same HR person who turned me down several times for the training roles! Once again, I sat before him and was ready to accept disappointment – only **this** time, the HR Director said, "You have been so persistent and have done so many things to prepare for the next role, you deserve a shot." He said he would recommend me for the interview.

To make a long story short, the process involved seven interviews with seven different leaders – *including* the VP of HR who was the Hiring Manager. When I entered his office, he offered me the position and stated that I had such overwhelming feedback, I actually set the standard for future candidates entering the program! I went on to complete the three-year program in **TWO** years and, upon graduation, was assigned to lead the HR team in a large facility where most graduates started off in smaller parts of the organization. The HRDP was my launching pad, and years later, I advanced to become a member of a Senior Human Resources Executive Team!

You never know where your passion will take you. God will strategically place you in situations that you may not immediately understand. Be open to challenges and willing to be flexible. Follow the tools and processes you have learned in this book and never settle for making it "there". Remember: Living your passion is a journey…not a destination.

Embrace a P2P lifestyle

I encourage you to develop a lifestyle focused on growth and development in every area of your life. This book focuses on moving from *Pain to Passion* – overcoming adversity. However, there are other P2P fundamentals you can embed within different seasons of your life in order to sustain a pain-free life. I'll share a few with you:

Prayer 2 Promise: In all things, keep God first. He has filled you with a purpose and promise for your life. Create a lifestyle of dialogue with Him and listen to His voice. I encourage you to study how you can become a more effective Prayer Warrior for Christ and begin to intercede on behalf of others. Remember: *It's not about you.*

Poised 2 Produce: Our society is filled with individuals who are "Jacks of all trades – and Masters of none". Spend some time honing in on your skills and become a 'Master' in your area of interest. Moving from mediocrity to a mastery mindset can be achieved through volunteerism, taking on additional 'stretch' assignments, or taking a leap of faith into unknown territories. Honing your skills will prepare you for the next level of opportunities that exist in and for your life.

Purge 2 Position: As you think about where you are today and where you want to be, are you in the right positon to receive and handle the blessings you seek? I encourage you to take time to purge – either semi-annually or annually. The Word of the Lord says:

"I am the true vine, and my Father is the gardener. He cuts off every branch in me that bears no fruit, while every branch that does bear fruit He prunes so that it will be even more fruitful. You are already clean because of the word I have spoken to you. Remain in me, as I also remain in you. No branch can bear fruit by itself; it must remain in the vine. Neither can you bear fruit unless you remain in me."

John 15:1-4

Purge those things you need to discard from your behavior, attitude, work ethic, relationships, financial practices, etc. Ask for constructive feedback and identify those areas that may derail or distract you from going to the next level. Then, create a 90-day plan to develop in those specific areas.

Praise 2 Prosper: Did you know that your praise is a weapon that can be used to defeat the enemy? Study God's Word and learn how to wage warfare against the enemy in your home, your health, and on your job. Learn how to build your faith. Incorporate positive affirmations into your daily routine. Allow your life to become an aroma that fills God's nostrils so that He will say He is well-pleased.

Provide 2 People: Become a conduit of God's blessings in the Earth. Take time to ensure you do not become constipated with the wisdom, knowledge, and resources you have gained over time. Be transparent and seek out ways to help someone - either through philanthropy, ministry, counseling, or simply taking the time to share your story. Seek ways to give back and pull someone else up and nurture their passion. As you duplicate yourself through others, your legacy will be established in the Earth.

Be Grateful

You may have endured **pain** at various points in your life, but if you are reading or listening to this book today, *you are still here*! Embed gratitude into your lifestyle and recognize that God has given you another opportunity to pursue your passion. *"And God shall wipe away all tears from their eyes; and there shall be no more death, neither sorrow, nor crying, neither shall there be any more pain: for the former things are passed away"* (Revelation 21:4 KJV). In all things give thanks, live your passion, and fulfill your purpose!

Purpose ...

Thank you, god, for what you have given;
The substance of my being that keeps me driven

Toward a goal with such great reward -
As long as I just keep on pressing forward

And striving to walk with an upfront gait.
With you as my guide, I will no longer wait

For someone else to claim my prize;
Through your word, O' Lord, you have opened my
eyes -

And now I can see what the future will hold.
You write the script for my life to unfold;

I will carry your wisdom and knowledge inside
In faithful application, the seed will multiply.

And my life will be worth so much more
Because through me will your blessings pour

Out into others whose lives are in need
Of your saving grace and mercy seed.

I will no longer ponder, "Lord, what shall I do?"
But become the vessel for your light to shine through;

And every day that I do your will,
My life has a meaning and purpose to fulfill.

Nikki Cheree

NOTES

CONNECT ON SOCIAL MEDIA

Nikki Cheree

@NikkiCheree1

@NikkiCheree1

Nikki_Cheree1

www.ingramcontent.com/pod-product-compliance
Lightning Source LLC
LaVergne TN
LVHW021342080426
835508LV00020B/2068